BE KIND!

AN ACTIVITY BOOK FOR YOUNG PEOPLE WHO CARE ABOUT OTHERS

STUDIO
PRESS

© 2019 Studio Press

Written by Stephanie Clarkson
Illustrated by Katie Abey
Designed by Rob Ward
Edited by Frankie Jones

978-1-78741-463-1
Printed in China   0240119
1 3 5 7 9 10 8 6 4 2

An imprint of Kings Road Publishing
Part of Bonnier Books UK
The Plaza, 535 King's Road, London, SW10 0SZ
www.studiopressbooks.co.uk
www.bonnierbooks.co.uk

THIS BOOK BELONGS TO

_____

WELCOME TO BE KIND!

This book will help you on your way to becoming a global citizen – in other words a kind, positive human being who cares about and wants the best for both the world and it's many different inhabitants.

Global citizenship is really important because when people think of themselves as being alike and really care about what happens to each other they're more likely to live peacefully and happily alongside each other.

You don't need to travel around the world to be a global citizen; you can do it simply by learning to think about the world as a whole, rather than just the part of it you live in and the people in your life like your family and friends.

The first step to thinking in this way is kindness – kindness to ourselves, to others and to our planet. This book is full of ideas to help you think about the world you live in and to be kinder.

Read through the checklist on the next page. Return to it from time to time as you complete the activities in this book, then tick off any statements that now apply to you as you journey towards global citizenship.

I AM A GLOBAL CITIZEN BECAUSE I...

... am curious about the world we live in and want to learn more about it. ☐

... try to understand and empathise with other people around the world and the issues that affect them. ☐

... believe that all people are equal and that no individual or group is better than others. ☐

... accept that people are unique and different. ☐

... am never unfriendly or mean to those who are different from me. ☐

... look after the environment through schemes like recycling. ☐

... know that I can make a positive difference in the world through my words and actions – however small. ☐

... use my voice to speak up about things that are unjust or not right in this world, and to spread positive and important messages. ☐

... act responsibly in my community, planning and carrying out positive actions to help improve life for other people. ☐

ONE WORLD

How much do you know about our world?

Start by finding the part of the world you live in, then complete the statements opposite about other places you know about or have visited. Spend some time thinking about areas of the world you're less familiar with.

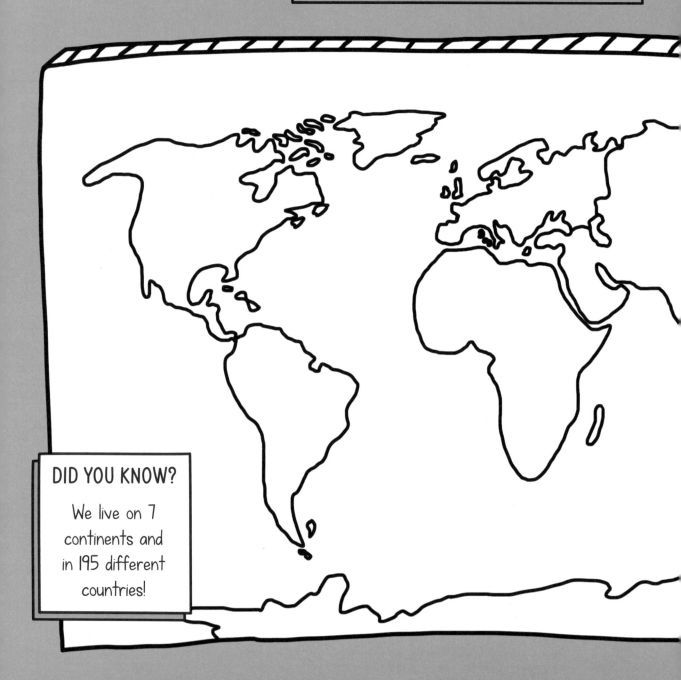

DID YOU KNOW?

We live on 7 continents and in 195 different countries!

DID YOU KNOW?

You're one of the 7.6 billion people in the world who make up the global community.

ADD THE COUNTRY NAME AND COLOUR IN THE AREAS OF THE MAP FOR EACH POINT BELOW:

I have visited _____

I have been on holiday to _____

I have friends in _____

I have family in _____

I would most like to travel to
_____

I know a cool fact about the people in
_____

I would love to know more about
_____

THE GIFT OF KINDNESS

Kindness is like a gift – it can be given to another person. Think about the kind things people have said or done for you, or that you have done for others.

Write the kind gifts on these packages.

One has been filled in as an example.

To: MY TEACHER

From: ME

I HELD THE CLASSROOM DOOR OPEN.

To:

From:

To:

From:

To:................
From:................

To:................
From:................

KINDNESS TAKES LOTS OF DIFFERENT FORMS.

It can be a thought, a word or an action.

It could be something small, like a smile, or bigger,
like standing up for someone who is being bullied.

KIND THOUGHT

There's a new boy in my class. I hope he is not feeling too nervous.

KIND WORD

"Hello, nice to meet you. Welcome to our class."

KIND ACTION

"I will show you the lunch hall so you don't get lost."

A FUNNY FEELING INSIDE

How does it feel when someone is kind to you?

Do you feel warm? Tingly? Fuzzy?

Draw or write down some words to show how kindness makes you feel on this picture.

Now think about how you feel inside when someone is unkind to you and use words or colours to show this.

BEHAVIOUR BOTHER

When someone says or does something unkind, it can make you feel sad, bad or angry. Being unkind to someone can make you feel negative emotions, too. You may also feel guilty for your actions.

Look at the people below.

Draw a line between the matching thought and speech bubbles.

YOU ARE REALLY RUBBISH AT RUNNING.

YOU HAVE NO FRIENDS!

I'm worried that Elsa might pick on me next.

I'm not sure if people really like me.

ONLY BABIES AREN'T ALLOWED TO PLAY OUT IN THE PARK AFTER SCHOOL.

I wish I didn't have to stay out, but I don't really want to go home because Mum and Dad aren't getting on.

I wish I could run as fast as you.

ELSA SAYS NO ONE SHOULD TALK TO YOU BECAUSE YOU'RE SNEAKY.

It is important to understand that you are not a bad person just because you have said or done something negative.

The important thing is to apologise and to do things differently next time.

It can be difficult but useful to think about your own mistakes. Write down some of the unkind things you have said or done in the past on the ticker tape. Think about how the other person felt, any consequences of your unkindness and what you have learned since.

WHAT CAN WE LEARN ABOUT OURSELVES?

Being unkind is often a reaction to anger within ourselves. It's important not to take unkindness personally, but nor do you have to tolerate it. Take some time to look at yourself, and think about when and why you've been unkind.

IN THEIR SHOES

People often use the word 'empathy' in relation to kindness. Empathy is when you're able to understand and care about how someone else feels.

SAY YOU'RE WALKING ALONG WITH SOMEONE AND THEY TRIP OVER...

... you might laugh at them, which would be unkind.

... you might help them up, which would be kind.

... or you might check they were okay because you might be thinking about how you once tripped over and how it was embarrassing and how much it hurt. You can sympathise because you can imagine just how that feels and you felt bad for them. This would be empathy.

Empathy differs from kindness in that it is the ability to put yourself in someone else's shoes and understand what they are going through. Empathy is important because if you can see things from another person's point of view you're more likely to treat them as you would wish to be treated.

Look at these footprints.

One foot shows a situation.

On the empty foot, write a reaction where you would be showing empathy towards the person.

Robert didn't get picked for the football team.

I will think about how sad Robert feels because he loves playing football.

Mum has been at work all day.

Sahir's parents are arguing.

I will think about how tired Mum will feel when she comes home from work after a long day.

Charlie is moving away.

Mo's hamster has died.

Eva is starting a new school.

COLOUR THIS IN:

BE THE
REASON
SOMEONE
SMILES!

THE COLOUR OF KIND

If kindness were a colour, what would it be?
Use pens or pencils to bring this page to life.
Alternatively, you could create a colour collage with
swatches of material or clippings from magazines.

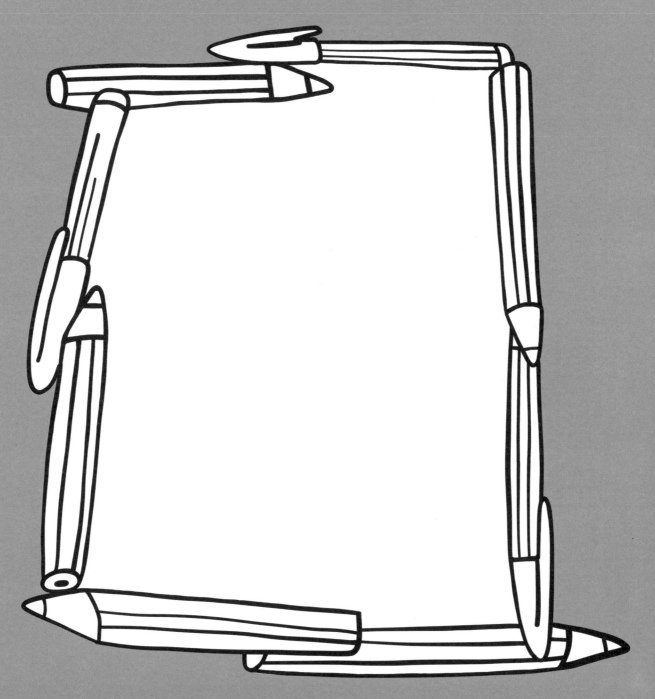

LISTEN, HEAR

Understanding others is key to global citizenship. You can only do this if you're listening to what others are saying and thinking about how they're feeling.

Make a vow to be a better listener and follow these tips.

WHEN SOMEONE IS SPEAKING...

Allow moments of silence so the person can think about what they're saying – don't jump in when they pause.

Keep your own past experiences to one side and really hear what the person is saying. If they are talking about how they have fallen out with a friend, it may be very different from the time you fell out with your friend.

Try to keep eye contact with the person, even if they are looking away while speaking.

When the person has finished talking, repeat what has been said. This will help the information sink into your brain and show the person that you really have listened to them.

Now set yourself a task and listen to three people. Write down something that they shared in the box opposite.

Today I listened to...

I found out...

Remember! If someone has said something you disagree with (a cruel comment about someone, for example), you should feel confident to speak up about it. Ensure they have finished talking and then explain that you don't agree with or appreciate their comment.

GIVE A GLOW

Compliments are like shooting stars – they light up someone's day and leave a glowing trail.

Learning to give and receive compliments takes practice. Write some compliments you could give on the tails of these stars.

"That's a pretty dress!"

STUCK FOR IDEAS?

"You are really good at football."

MY PEEPS

Fill the picture frames with drawings of people you know.

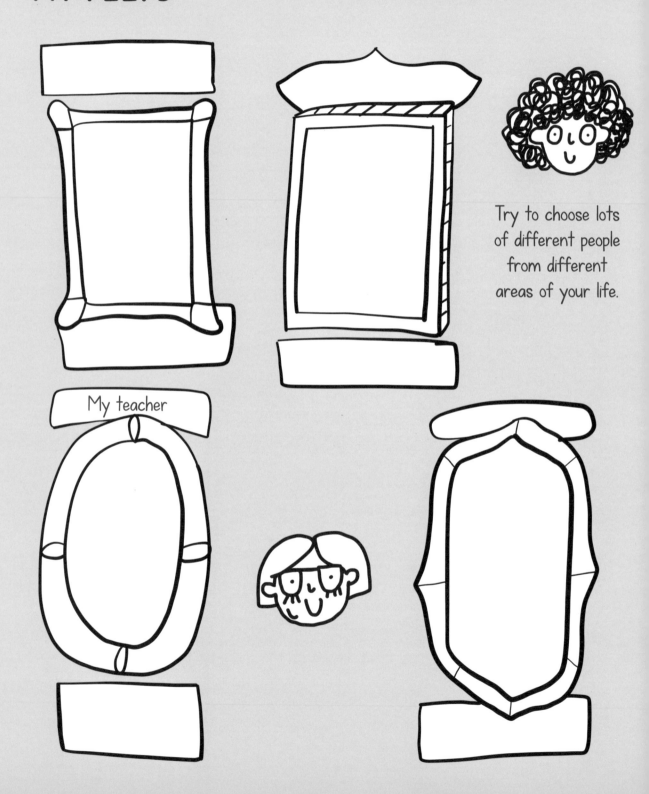

Try to choose lots of different people from different areas of your life.

My teacher

Write down your favourite thing about each person in the space below the picture.

Always makes
me laugh

Is a kind friend

HEAR ME ROAR

Being kind can take courage, especially if you are up against a group of people who are being mean to someone.

Draw a lion on this page to inspire you and remind you to be brave enough to be kind.

TAKE ACTION!

What could you say or do when others are being unkind?

If I heard a rumour about someone in my class, I would...

- -

If I saw a group of people leaving someone out, I would...

- -

If I saw someone stealing someone's lunch money, I would...

- -

PRACTISE POSITIVITY

Think of two things you could say to each person to make them feel good.

1.

2.

1.

2.

1.

2.

1.

2.

SPREAD THE JOY: SMILE STONES

Smile stones are a great craft activity and a brilliant way to make someone's day.

They are rocks or stones decorated with positive pictures or messages and gifted or left for people to find.

YOU WILL NEED:

- Large flat stones or pebbles
- Washing up liquid
- Paper towel or a tea towel
- Old newspapers
- Permanent markers
- Acrylic paint
- Paintbrush
- Clear acrylic top coat (optional)

1. Collect lots of rocks or large stones from your garden. If you don't have a garden, you could buy the rocks from a craft store. Make sure each rock has a flat or gently curved surface.

2. Wash the stones clean of any dirt, mud or sand with water and washing-up liquid.

3. Pat dry with paper towels or a tea towel, or leave to dry in the sun.

Always ask an adult's permission before starting a craft activity.

4. Lay the old newspapers on the surface you are planning to work on – these will protect the surface from the paint or varnish.

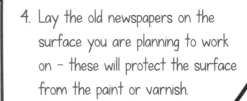

5. Paint your stones with fun, friendly pictures – a smiley face, a unicorn, a strawberry – or words – joy, peace, love, hope, friend. These could be anything you like, but think about how they would brighten someone's day.

6. Leave the rocks to dry after each coat or layer of paint or pen.

7. Once dry, take outside and lay on newspaper. Paint or spray with a clear top coat to protect from the sun.

8. Give the rocks to friends, family members or people you think might need a little kindness. You could also leave them around for people to find. Alternatively, you could ask your school or community group if you could make a positivity garden, featuring lots of rocks.

CHALK IT UP!

Want a quick and easy way to spread joy? Grab some coloured chalk and write uplifting quotes or messages on pavements for passers-by to read.

SMILING IS CONTAGIOUS

A heartfelt smile is the first step on the road to kindness. Smiling is a simple way to brighten anyone's day. It is also contagious. The more you smile, the more you'll make others smile.

Draw a smile on each face once you've given each of these grin-tastic activities a try.

Smile at someone who is not in your school year.

Smile when you walk into a shop.

Smile a greeting to a neighbour.

Smile at your teacher.

Smile while you talk on the phone, even though they can't see you!

Smile at the person who delivers your post.

STUCK FOR SMILES?

On a separate piece of paper, write down five silly things that have happened this week and share the funny stories with anyone who needs a giggle.

SOMEONE LIKE ME

The world's a big place, so you might not often think about people who live far away.

Choose a country you have never visited and do some research about what life is like in that country for children of your age.

Now complete the illustration of a child born in that country and add some facts about the child's life. Think about how life is different for them. In what ways do you think you might be similar?

FACTS

Our lives might be different because...

1.

2.

3.

We could be similar because...

1.

2.

3.

PEN FRIENDS

Imagine you have a pen pal in another country.
You could think about the person you imagined on the last page,
or pick someone from a different place altogether.

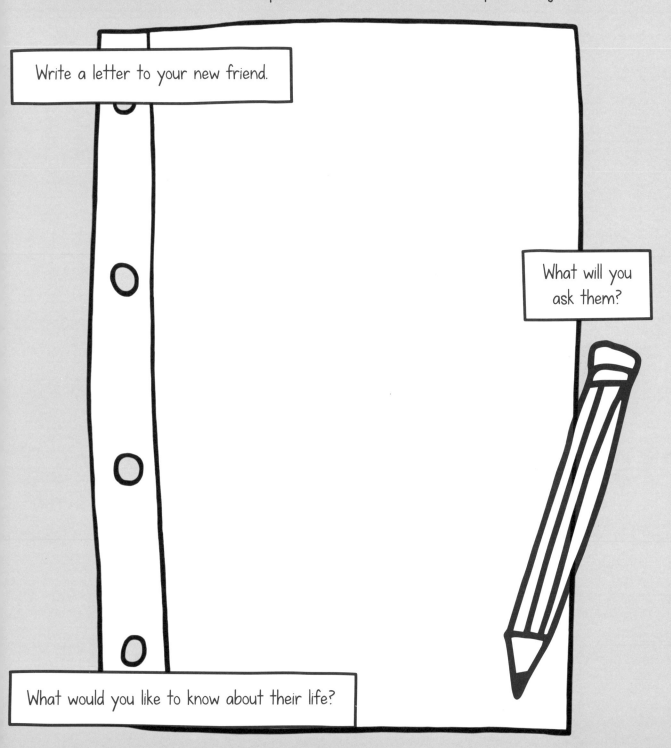

Write a letter to your new friend.

What will you ask them?

What would you like to know about their life?

ANYTIME GIFT

Grab a jar or box, add stickers or a ribbon and fill it throughout the year with items to make someone smile.

Presents can extend beyond Christmas or birthdays. In fact, gifts involving long-term thought and planning are exceptionally kind.

YOU COULD ADD...

Fun sayings or quotes.

Pretty shells or stones.

Memories about a person.

A poem or song.

Small change from your pocket money.

A book you enjoyed reading.

Lovely pictures cut from magazines.

FOR EXTRA IMPACT YOU COULD LEAVE THIS AS A SURPRISE FOR THE GIFT'S RECIPIENT.

GOOD CHOICES

Every day we are faced with situations and we have to make choices.

We can choose to do the kind thing or we can go the other way.

THIS IS LILY

Think through the situations below and complete them with a drawing to show either the good or bad choice she could make.

BAD CHOICES  **SITUATION** **GOOD CHOICES**

HERE IS THE NEWS

Adults should turn to the back of the book for information about how to talk through difficult issues before beginning this activity.

TALKING TIPS!

Take some time to watch the news or read a newspaper with a grown-up, a parent or a guardian.

Pick one story that interests you or makes you feel sad or angry.

Talk about it with them. Think about how any children affected might feel.

How will you help? Add some ways you think you could make a difference.

Write to an authority figure in your country such as a councillor or politician.

_ _ _ _ _ _ _ _ _ _ _ _
_ _ _ _ _ _ _ _ _ _ _ _
_ _ _ _ _ _ _ _ _ _ _ _
_ _ _ _ _ _ _ _ _ _ _ _

Pen a thank-you letter to a company that is working to protect our planet, or write to a global organisation that has room for improvement. Tell them your thoughts.

_ _ _ _ _ _ _ _ _ _ _ _
_ _ _ _ _ _ _ _ _ _ _ _
_ _ _ _ _ _ _ _ _ _ _ _
_ _ _ _ _ _ _ _ _ _ _ _
_ _ _ _ _ _ _ _ _ _ _ _
_ _ _ _ _ _ _ _ _ _ _ _

Tell others about the issue with a presentation or Show and Tell at school.

_ _ _ _ _ _ _ _ _ _ _ _
_ _ _ _ _ _ _ _ _ _ _ _
_ _ _ _ _ _ _ _ _ _ _ _
_ _ _ _ _ _ _ _ _ _ _ _
_ _ _ _ _ _ _ _ _ _ _ _
_ _ _ _ _ _ _ _ _ _ _ _

SPEAK OUT

One of the best ways to make people feel that they are part of the global community is through great communication.

Use this page to plan a letter or speech about the issue in the news story you picked out in the previous activity.

MAKE A CARE PACKAGE

A care package is a great way to show someone you're thinking about them.

You could give it to a friend, a family member or someone in your community.

Here's what to do...

YOU WILL NEED:

- A basket, box or shoebox
- PVA glue
- Scissors, to be used under supervision
- Old and unwanted magazines, wrapping paper, greeting cards, etc.
- Items to make the person smile (there are some ideas on the next page!)

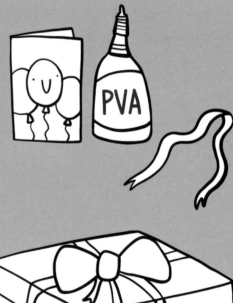

1. First, concentrate on the package itself. You could line a basket with fabric and tie on pieces of ribbon. Alternatively, decorate the outside of a shoebox or cardboard box with a collage of wonderful pictures cut from old magazines, gift wrap or greetings cards. Simply glue on and make sure they overlap to ensure the entire box is covered.

2. Leave to dry.

3. Now comes the fun bit. Fill your box or basket with items to bring a smile to the face of the person who will be receiving the care package. It's up to you what you include, but always check with a parent or guardian first.

4. Check your package through with a grown-up and then it's ready to give to your chosen person.

YOU COULD INCLUDE:

- A lovely photograph of you and the recipient
- A notebook and pen
- A home-made card
- A necklace or bracelet made from beads or pasta shells
- A handwritten memory
- A quote from the person's favourite book
- A picture made from your handprints – try a bunch of flowers using your handprints as the petals
- A list of activities you'd like to do with the person next time you see them
- A pretty piece of colourful ribbon
- A badge or button

YOU ARE AWESOME

Use this page to write a letter or note to someone to show your appreciation.

Think about all the things that make them great and say a heartfelt thank you!

WE GO TOGETHER

Because the world's such a big place, it's easy to think we have nothing in common with people who live far away. So, how do you fit into the world? Connect the labels below to each circle to discover how we all fit together.

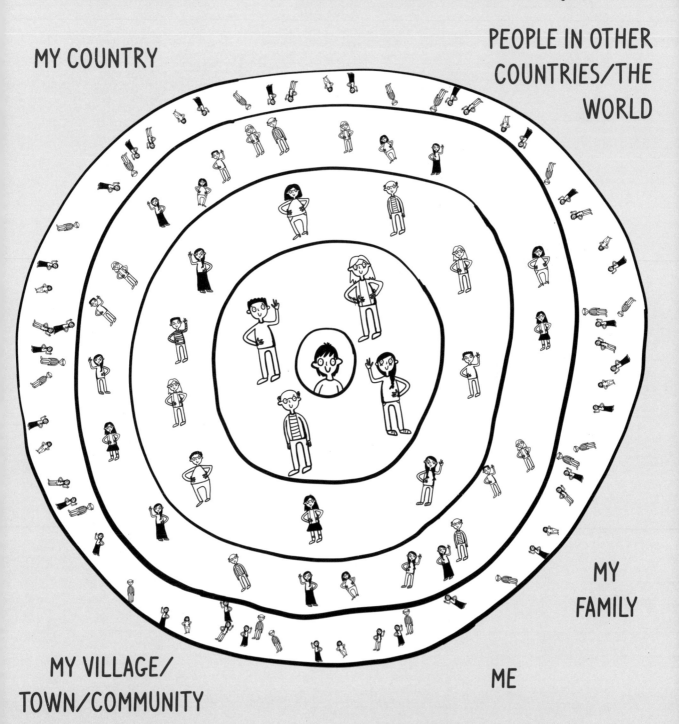

MY COUNTRY

PEOPLE IN OTHER COUNTRIES/THE WORLD

MY FAMILY

MY VILLAGE/ TOWN/COMMUNITY

ME

KINDNESS BEGINS AT HOME

Write down or draw six things you could do to help the people you live with and add them to this home.

COMMUNITY MATTERS

A community is a group of people living in the same place or having a particular belief or interest in common.

Use this page to think about the communities you are involved with.

Think about the ways you spend your time – your school, your hobbies, your village or town. Pick one community and write about it.

NAME:

AGE:

THE COMMUNITY I AM PART OF IS:

I ENJOY BELONGING TO THIS COMMUNITY BECAUSE:

THE ONE THING I WOULD CHANGE ABOUT IT IS:

THE INJUSTICES IN MY COMMUNITY ARE:

THINK CAREFULLY!

INJUSTICES ARE THINGS THAT AREN'T RIGHT OR FAIR. FOR EXAMPLE...

Perhaps children aren't allowed to play ball in the local park.

Perhaps there is a boys-only football team and nothing offered for girls.

Maybe the school trip offered at your school is expensive, which means that some people cannot go.

Maybe people in younger years in your school are not allowed to sit on the school council.

ACTION PLAN

Plan an event to bring your community together. This could be to raise funds for a particular group or need within the community.

Or, it could just be a way to get people together and communicating.

Take a look at some of the ideas below. Who could you involve?

What would you need to do to make this happen? Write your action plan down on a sheet of paper.

WHY NOT ORGANISE A...

JUMBLE SALE

BAKE SALE

SPONSORED WALK

PET SHOW

MUSIC CONCERT OR PLAY

WINTER FUN AFTERNOON — SLEDGING RACES, SNOWBALL FIGHTS, SNOWMAN-BUILDING

COLOUR THIS IN:

I CHOOSE KIND

DIFFERENT BUT THE SAME

Different is good. It's what makes the world interesting.

We often like or love other people precisely because they are not the same as us.

Pick someone at school or in your family who you feel is different from you.

WHO I CHOSE:

Write down some of the things that make you different from each other.

WHAT MAKES US DIFFERENT:

Now write down some of the things that make you the same.

WHAT MAKES US THE SAME:

Which of these things really help you to like or love that person?

Think about the things that make us different from each other…

Physical appearance –
eye, skin and hair colour, height…

Hobbies and interests

Religion

Who they love

Customs and traditions –
wearing special items of clothing
or eating certain things…

Do you have a friend who is different from you in the way they
are or in the way they think about things?

What do you know about their beliefs or lifestyle?

KINDNESS WREATH

Want to remind yourself that the world is full of kindness? This stylish wreath is built on acts of kindness.

The more kindness you observe in the world, the bigger the wreath grows. It is also simple and fun to make, and brightens up any room.

YOU WILL NEED:

- A wire or wooden wreath frame from a craft store or garden centre (optional)
- Coloured ribbon

- An empty jar
- Scissors, to be used under adult supervision
- Glue

OR FOR A HOME-MADE WREATH FRAME:

- Stiff card
- A dinner plate

- Pencil
- Or pipe cleaners

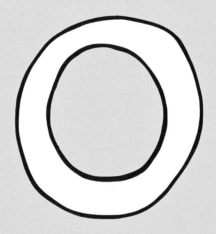

1. You will need a frame on which to make your wreath. You can either buy a wire or wooden frame from a craft store or garden centre, or make your own.

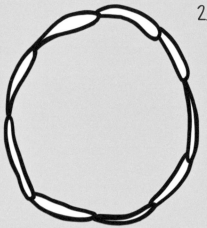

2. If making your own frame, you could knot several pipe cleaners together to make a circle or, for a card frame, lay a dinner plate on the stiff card and draw around the circle with a pencil. Mark points 2–3 cm inside the circle as markers for the inner rim. Join those together. Finally, cut out the circles to give yourself an 'o' shape.

Always ask an adult's permission before starting a craft activity.

3. Spend some time with your family cutting up thin scraps of ribbon or fabric. The more types and colours of ribbon you have, the better the wreath will look. The pieces of ribbon should be long enough that they can be tied around the wreath in a bow or knot.

4. Store your pieces of ribbon in a jar, ready for use.

5. Once you have your wreath, add a loop of ribbon to give you a way to hang it up.

6. It will look very plain at first but just wait... this will all change.

7. Every time you witness or do an act of kindness – however big or small – you should mark this by tying a piece of ribbon to your wreath. If you find your ribbons are slipping, you can fix them in place with a dot of glue to the underside of the ribbon.

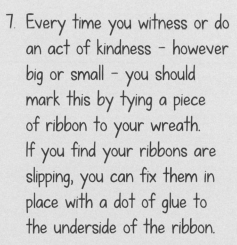

8. Continue to do this until your wreath is brimming with colour and none of the frame can be seen.

BLAST OFF

Fill this space-bound rocket up with things that make people unhappy or miserable and that aren't good or nice for the planet or its people. Choose things that the world would be better off without.

THINK CAREFULLY!

This isn't a question of sending your grumpy head teacher off into space!

Think about bigger issues, ones that negatively affect lots of people around the world, like HUNGER.

ALWAYS THERE

Some things in your life are literally 'on tap'.

This means that, like having running water coming straight from the tap, they happen automatically without you having to think about them.

Write down or draw some of the things you take for granted coming out of this tap.

Do you think there are some things you take for granted that some people might not have access to?

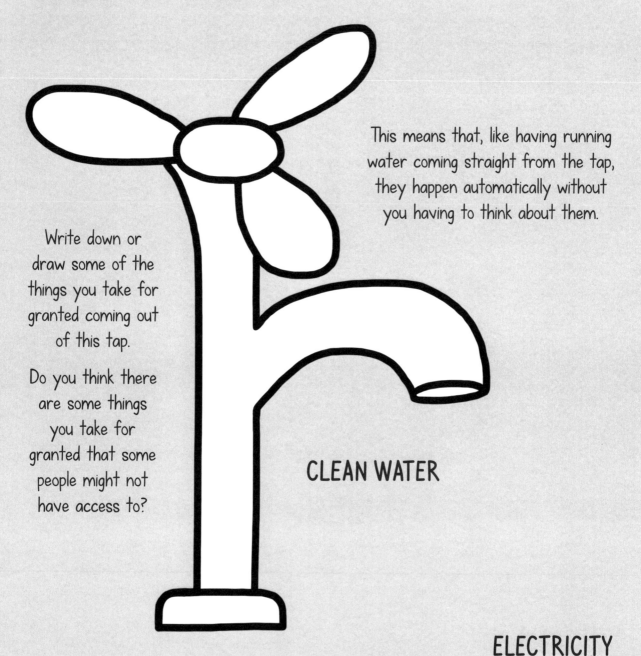

CLEAN WATER

ELECTRICITY

FOOD

JUST BECAUSE

Give someone an appreciative note for no reason.

Fill in the sticky notes with some ideas for positive messages you could write down and stick up for someone to find.

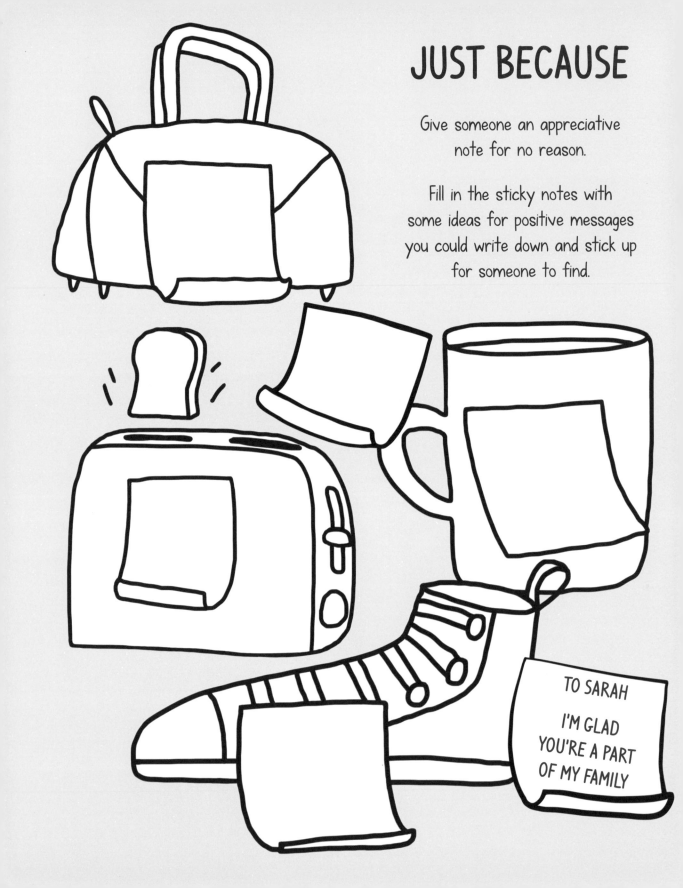

TO SARAH

I'M GLAD YOU'RE A PART OF MY FAMILY

ANIMAL INSTINCTS

If kindness or empathy were animals, how would they look?

DRAW THEM HERE.

Would they have fur, hair or feathers?

Would they be bright pink or a vibrant blue colour?

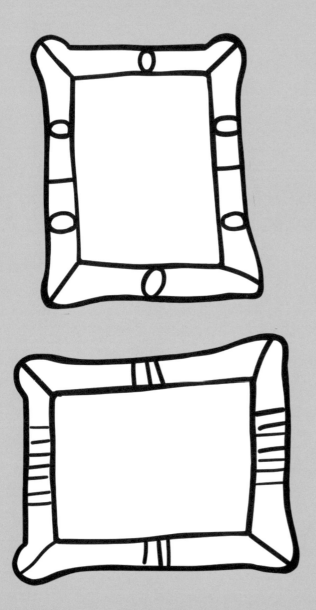

HUMAN RIGHTS

In 1989, world leaders decided that children under the age of 18 needed special care and protection.

They wanted to make sure the world recognised that children have human rights, too.

The countries in the United Nations signed a treaty called The Convention on the Rights of the Child.

The right to be treated without discrimination of any kind.

The right to play and enjoy rest and leisure time.

The right to good healthcare.

The right to practise the religion of your choice.

The right to the freedom of thought.

The right to be protected from people who would mistreat you and make you do things against your will.

You have many rights as a child.
Which of these do you feel most strongly about?

The right to education.

The right to nutritious food and clean drinking water.

The right not to have to fight in wars.

The right to special care and a full and healthy life, if disabled.

The right to enjoy your own culture.

The right to be presumed innocent if accused of a crime and not to be thrown into prison without a trial.

The right to survival.

Colour the panel behind each statement in if you think some people in the world might not have access to this right.

#CHOOSE KIND

With online bullying and social media issues often in the spotlight, it's easy to forget that technology can also be a force for good. Sending an email or a text message is a super-fast way to spread some joy.

Think about the people in your life and then write some short but positive messages on these screens.

WORD TO THE WISE!

Check with a trusted adult before sending text or online messages.

I HOPE

On the messages carried by these doves, write some of your hopes for the future when it comes to life and our planet.

CARING MEANS...

What does caring mean to you?

Use the capital letters to write an acrostic poem to remind yourself of the true meaning of the word. Each sentence you think of must begin with the capital letter on the page below.

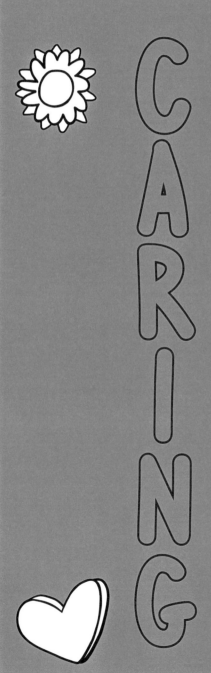

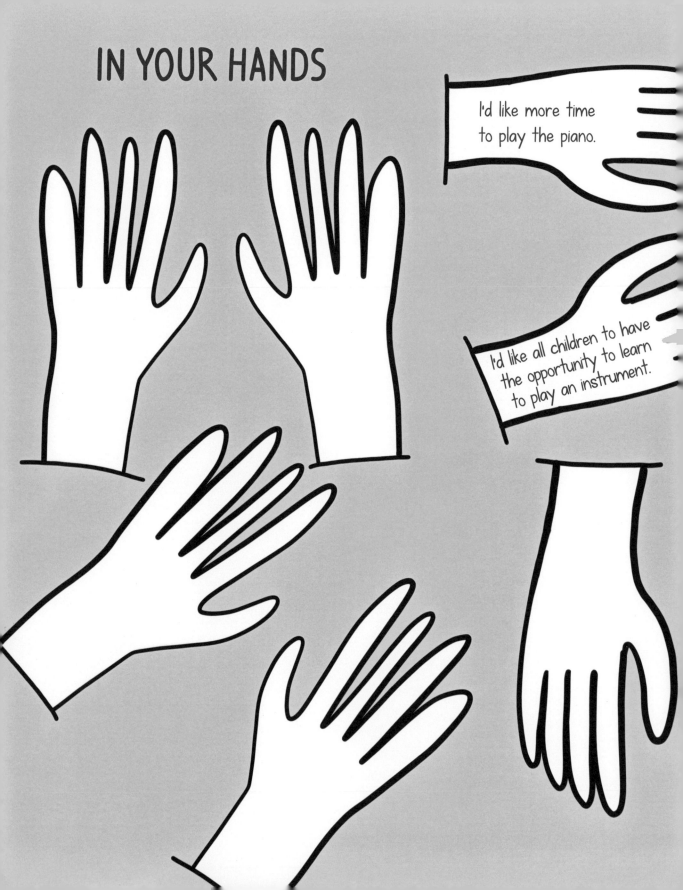

We have two hands, one for ourselves and one to help others.

Write something you'd like to do to help yourself on the palm of one hand and something you'd like to change for the benefit of others on the palm of the other hand.

TEAMWORK

Working together to achieve something is a great way to stop focusing on yourself and start thinking about others.

Grab some friends and try some of these team-building activities.

REMEMBER! THERE'S NO 'I' IN 'TEAM'!

HULA CHAIN

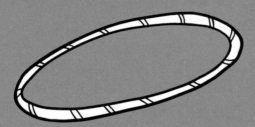

One person picks up a hula hoop and threads it onto one arm. Then, the group all hold hands in a circle. The aim is to get the hula hoop to travel around the circle to the starting point without anyone letting go of anyone's hand at any point.

CATEGORIES

One person calls out categories and the group has to arrange and rearrange itself according to those categories. It could be 'hair colour' or 'what you ate for breakfast' or 'age' or 'favourite hobbies'.

THE HUMAN KNOT

Get together in a tight group. On the count of three, everyone grabs someone else's wrist. Then you need to work out how to untangle yourselves without letting go.

PM FOR ONE DAY

Imagine you are prime minister for one day.

Use this page to write a kindness manifesto – a document showing your pledges (the things you promise to do) to make life better for people around the world.

IT IS TIME TO...

Too busy to be kind? Make time for others by swapping an activity you regularly do for yourself with something you could do for others in the same time frame.

Fill this swap table with ideas for kindly and timely swaps.

ACTIVITY	TIME	SWAP FOR
Playing on a computer or tablet	15 minutes	Calling a relative
Bouncing on the trampoline	10 minutes	Helping with the washing-up

WORLD HACKS

It's difficult to see how a small action can have such a huge impact on the world, but small actions build on each other once you take that first step.

Tick the things below when you have incorporated them into your life. Write down how they help and why, then colour the star once you've shared your knowledge with others.

☐ ⭐ Turn the tap off when you're brushing your teeth.

☐ ⭐ Have showers not baths.

☐ ⭐ Use the smaller flush on the toilet, if you have one.

☐ ⭐ Try a reusable food wrap for your packed lunch.

☐ ⭐ Use a refillable water bottle instead of a disposable one.

☐ ⭐ Help a tired bee with a teaspoon of sugared water.

REMEMBER TO TELL OTHERS ABOUT WHAT YOU ARE DOING, TO ENCOURAGE THEM TO FOLLOW YOUR EXAMPLE.

FUR AND FEATHERS

Animals are part of our world, too.

Whether you have a pet in the house or not, here are some ways to be kind to furry or four-legged friends.

ADD A PAW PRINT WHENEVER YOU DO ONE OF THE ACTIVITIES BELOW.

- [ ] Take a dog for a walk. (You could ask to walk a friend's dog or neighbour's dog!)

- [ ] Take five minutes to stroke a pet.

- [ ] Clean out a pet's bed or cage.

- [ ] Find a pet's favourite toy and play with them.

- [ ] Sponsor an endangered species.

- [ ] Take time to read about or research facts about your favourite animal.

- [ ] Feed the birds.

- [ ] Create an insect-friendly area.

- [ ] Offer to feed a neighbour's cat.

SWEET MUSIC

Think about some of the music tracks that make you feel good.

Write a song or create a pick-me-up playlist and dedicate it to someone who deserves a treat.

HURRAY FOR GIRLS

Strong girls grow into wonderful women. Colour in the characters, then write their names below the role they played in making the world a better, fairer place on the opposite page.

EMMELINE PANKHURST

MARIE CURIE

MARGARET HAMILTON

AMELIA EARHART

MALALA YUSAFZAI

ROSA PARKS

A British suffragette who campaigned for women to get the vote.

An American computer scientist who wrote the code that took man to the moon.

Refused to give up her bus seat for a white person. Fought for civil rights and race equality in the USA.

Helped to invent the X-ray and therefore helped in the fight against cancer.

A Pakistani schoolgirl who helped to raise awareness about the right to education in some countries in the world.

An American pilot who helped to raise the profile of women in aviation, and showed women to be brave and adventurous.

THERE ARE STILL MANY PLACES IN THE WORLD WHERE WOMEN DON'T ENJOY THE SAME RIGHTS AS MEN.

FIND OUT ABOUT THE COUNTRIES WHERE GENDER EQUALITY IS NOT PART OF THEIR CULTURE.

FIND THE KIND

Bad news sells, which is why the press is full of it.

However, in reality there are lots of uplifting things happening all the time.

Fill these front pages with some real-life good news stories.

SCHOOL'S COOL

School can seem like a drag, but in fact education is a privilege, as it allows us choices and opportunities in life.

THINK HARD.

Write down all the things that are good about your learning environment.

FRIENDS RULE

Friends are great, aren't they?

Grab one of your pals, two pens or pencils, and take a page each.

Now complete the sentences to help you to appreciate each others' qualities.

I really like your personality because...

Some adjectives that describe you are...

I look forward to seeing you because...

I know I can count on you when...

I really appreciate when you...

I am impressed by the way you...

One idea I've taken from you is...

I really like your personality because...

Some adjectives that describe you are...

I look forward to seeing you because...

I know I can count on you when...

I really appreciate when you...

I am impressed by the way you...

One idea I've taken from you is...

BUCKETS OF KINDNESS

Imagine you carry an invisible bucket around each day.

Use a pencil to fill each bucket with at least five good things you've done for or said to other people this week.

When you're done you can rub them out and start a fresh week.

BEING KIND REQUIRES A POSITIVE MINDSET

GET YOURSELF THERE BY COLOURING THESE WONDERFUL WORDS...

AMAZING   SUCCESSFUL   KIND

FASCINATING   BRAVE   BRIGHT

THOUGHTFUL   CONFIDENT

HOPEFUL   DESERVING   LOVING

FRIENDLY   CLEVER   FABULOUS

GENUINE   WONDERFUL

HELPFUL   HAPPY   AWESOME

MINDFUL   CAPABLE   GLOWING

WHAT IS IT LIKE TO...

Empathy means understanding.

To help you to empathise with people who don't have access to the things you take for granted, practise giving something up for a week.

Fill in this reverse star chart every time you do without something.

	MON	TUES	WED	THURS	FRI	SAT	SUN
COMPUTER OR TABLET							
TREATS (E.G. CINEMA, SPORTS)							
GAMES CONSOLE							
DESSERTS							
POCKET MONEY							
SNACKS							

CINEMA

THANK-YOU CARD

There's nothing more personal than a fingerprint.

Yours are unique to you.

Use them to make a card for someone you love or appreciate. Here's how…

YOU WILL NEED:

- Pencils
- Coloured card
- Glue stick
- Paint
- Pens
- White paper
- Scissors*

* USE SCISSORS UNDER SUPERVISION!

1. Fold the coloured card in half and decide if you want your card to be landscape or portrait.

2. On the white paper, mark out a rectangle that is slightly smaller than the front dimensions of the card.

3. Cut it out.

4. Glue the white paper onto the card and leave to dry.

6. Now you're ready to add your fingerprints. To make a fingerprint, pour some paint into a dish. Dip the tip of your finger into the paint. Press it on a scrap of paper once to remove the excess paint, then press your finger carefully onto the paper. Keep still and make sure you remove your finger straight up into the air afterwards, to avoid smudging.

YOU COULD MAKE…

- a multicoloured caterpillar – 'Thank you!'

- a collection of flowers – 'Thanks a bunch'

- a thumb-print dandelion clock – 'It's time… to say a big thank you!'

- a swarm of bees – 'Thank you for bee-ing you!'

- some print people, holding hands – 'Thank you for everything!'

LOVING IS GIVING

There's a lot of love in the world.

Fill this page with beautiful hearts of all shapes and sizes, then colour them in.

ONLY THE LONELY

Lots of different people can feel lonely.

Can you remember the last time you felt lonely?

What did it feel like?

Draw how loneliness might feel on this page.

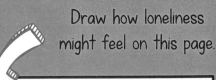

Does loneliness feel like a big hole?

Does it feel like a tiny rabbit?

Elderly people often feel lonely.

Are there any ways you could help an older person in your family or your community?

Write your ideas below...

If you were feeling lonely, what would make you feel better?

I COULD: _

_ _

_ _

_ _

_ _

WORLD KINDNESS DAY

Did you know that kindness has it's own celebration day? World Kindness Day is celebrated around the globe on 13th November every year.

13 NOV

Mark your calendar to remind you of this forthcoming date, then spend the day being extra caring and thoughtful. Complete the diary entry detailing your kind actions on that day.

WORLD KINDNESS DAY
was launched in 1998 by The World Kindness Movement, which is made up of 28 nations. The mission of this day is to inspire individuals and nations to create a kinder world.

ME, ME, ME

You deserve kindness, too. Begin by finding ways to be kinder to yourself.

Draw a self-portrait and write down three things you could do for yourself.

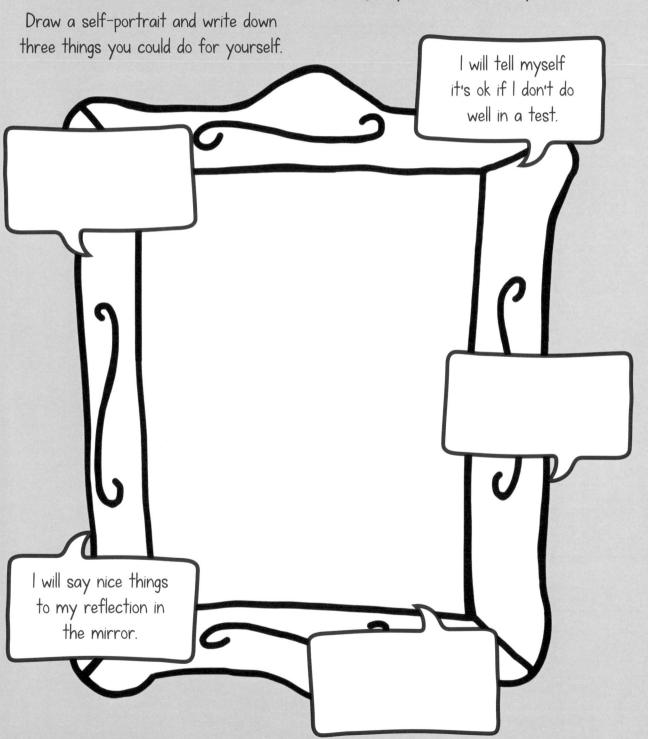

TAKE NOTICE

Have you ever noticed that there are many people who come into your life and help you in a small way?

Draw them under the magnifying glasses.

Give yourself one week to really look in detail at those people, from the person who serves your school lunch, to the person who delivers your post or the people who collect your bins.

ACCEPTING OTHERS

Accepting other people is key to being a global citizen.

It involves learning not to label others, or judge them for the way they look, how they choose to live or what they believe, even if they are very different from you.

Sign the pledge to remind you to accept others.

I,

_ _ _ _ _ _ _ _ _ _ ,

PLEDGE TO LEARN TO ACCEPT
PEOPLE FOR WHO THEY ARE,
NOT WHO I WANT THEM TO BE!

SIGNED:

_ _ _ _ _ _ _ _ _ _

POVERTY

Poverty affects millions of people across the globe.

It can be difficult to see how you can help with such a huge issue, but being a global citizen means you find out more and take action where possible.

Do some research into what poverty means, then colour in a letter for every action you take.

 P Clean out your wardrobe or toy box and donate unwanted items to those in need, through a goodwill charity.

 O Find items you don't want any more and, with help and permission from a grown-up, sell them online.

 V Remind your parents to go out and vote for candidates who promise to work to ease poverty.

Give a talk at school about poverty and how it affects people. **E**

 E

R Give your support to businesses, organisations and laws that protect people living in poverty.

 T Take a stand against prejudice by always treating people for who they are, not what they have. For example, don't avoid being someone's friend just because their clothes are out of style or different to yours.

 Y Educate yourself about children in the UK who are growing up in poverty. Make a decision to feel lucky and blessed.

DID YOU KNOW?

POVERTY IS DEFINED IN DIFFERENT WAYS...

ABSOLUTE POVERTY — When people don't have enough money to meet basic needs to help them survive, such as food, shelter and access to healthcare.

RELATIVE POVERTY — When people earn much less money than the average in their country. People living in relative poverty in the UK, for example, would still have more money than those living in relative poverty in other developing countries.

PAY IT FORWARD

We're often told that 'one good deed deserves another', but paying it forward involves doing a good deed, or spreading some love to others, without expecting anything in return, rather than paying someone back for being kind.

It feels good to pass on some good feelings to other people. Here are some ways to do just that.

MAKE A TOKEN SYSTEM

TAKE A SMILE

Take a piece of paper or card and section off some wishes or smiles with dotted lines. Make a cut on the dotted line to form a tab that can be torn off. Stick this up on a school noticeboard, on a tree or even on your kitchen fridge, so that people can tear one off and help themselves to good wishes or smiles.

CHAIN REACTION

Send a positive message in a handwritten note or via email. Pass it on to someone. Make sure you write something to make people feel happy, like 'FIND THE GOOD'.

CHANGE FOR CHANGE

Collect any spare change from your pocket money and keep it in a jar. When it is full, add a sticker to the front saying 'coins for anyone who needs them' and leave it somewhere public where people might not have the coins they need.

You could leave it near a car park ticket machine, for example.

NOT GETTING ON

We can't always agree. Fill these comic strips with ideas about the kind of flare-ups that happen in your life and community.

What do you think you could do to calm the situation and help to resolve each conflict?

HURRAH FOR BOYS...

Colour in the images of these amazing men and write their names beneath the actions that made them great role models on the opposite page

In the past, boys were sometimes told not to show their emotions and they were expected to fit in, but many dared to be different.

LIONEL MESSI

JOHN LENNON

MUHAMMAD ALI

ALAN TURING

MARTIN LUTHER KING JR

WILLIAM KAMKWAMBA

Argentinian football star with a social conscience who donates lots of his time and money to the United Nations Children's Fund (UNICEF). He also has his own charitable foundation that supports access to healthcare, education and sport for children.

Minister and activist who helped to fight racial inequality in a peaceful way. He helped to organise marches and his 'I Have a Dream' speech about the importance of treating each other as equals is very famous.

Inventor from Malawi who, despite having to drop out of school because of the severe famine in his country, used the local library to study. As a result, he became interested in science and the use of energy. He went on to invent a windmill system to power houses and pump water, and now works as a design engineer on projects to help poor communities in developing countries.

Musician from Liverpool who campaigned for peace and equality. He showed courage in standing up to the US president, when he spoke out against his foreign policy.

American boxer who worked for various causes and donated millions to charity organisations to help refugees in countries like Rwanda. He also helped to negotiate the release of hostages in the Middle East.

Computer scientist and mathematician who helped win the Second World War through his work in cracking codes. He fell in love with men and was treated badly by the British government for this. He was granted a pardon after his death and there is a law in his name to help others who were badly treated in their lifetimes.

KINDNESS CHEQUE BOOK

Use the templates below to plan some tokens for someone, thinking carefully about things you could promise to do to make their life easier.

Once you're happy, create your own on blank paper. Cut them out and staple them together to make a booklet, or present them in a gift box or jar.

Make a book of promises for a family member who works hard on your behalf.

This coupon entitles
the bearer to...
... ONE LIE-IN

I solemnly promise to...

I solemnly promise to...

This coupon entitles
the bearer to...

_____
_____
_____
_____

This coupon entitles
the bearer to...
_____
_____

I solemnly promise to...
_____
_____
_____

_____
_____
_____

This coupon entitles
the bearer to...
_____
_____

I solemnly promise to...
_____
_____

_____
_____
_____

_____
_____

SUPERPOWER

Imagine you have the power to grant wishes to help people.

You can give anything or do anything for anyone, but not in a material way.

Write someone's name and the thing you'd do for them on every symbol.

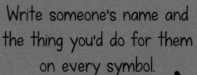

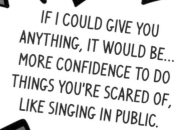

IF I COULD GIVE YOU ANYTHING, IT WOULD BE... MORE CONFIDENCE TO DO THINGS YOU'RE SCARED OF, LIKE SINGING IN PUBLIC.

IF I COULD GIVE YOU ANYTHING IT WOULD BE... HALF AN HOUR EXTRA EACH DAY SO YOU COULD HAVE A LOVELY BATH.

RAK BINGO

Play a game of RAK Bingo with a friend or family member.

Copy this card for them to take away.

The aim of the game is to cross out each Random Act of Kindness when you have done it.

First to do every act has a full house and wins.

VISIT SOMEONE WHO IS SICK	WRITE A HANDWRITTEN LETTER TO SOMEONE	HELP AN ELDERLY PERSON TO CROSS THE STREET	WALK A NEIGHBOUR'S DOG
GIVE UP YOUR SEAT ON THE BUS OR TRAIN	GIVE SOMEONE A HUG	DO SOMETHING NEIGHBOURLY - TAKE IN A PARCEL, WATER THEIR PLANTS OR PUT OUT THEIR BINS	HELP TO PREPARE A MEAL FOR SOMEONE
HOLD THE DOOR OPEN FOR SOMEONE ELSE	HELP SOMEONE WHO IS STRUGGLING WITH HEAVY BAGS/SHOPPING	SHARE YOUR UMBRELLA ON A RAINY DAY	SAY THANK YOU WITH A GIFT
GIVE DIRECTIONS	PICK UP LITTER	OFFER SOME OLD BOOKS TO A HOSPITAL OR DOCTORS' WAITING ROOM	LET SOMEONE GO IN FRONT OF YOU IN A QUEUE

BE A RAKTIVIST

Are you a Raktivist? RAK stands for Random Act of Kindness and is something selfless you do for someone else, without thought of being paid or how you might benefit from doing it.

I COULD ASK MY FRIEND IF THEY WOULD LIKE HELP WITH THEIR HOMEWORK.

On these pages are some RAK scenarios.

Think how you can help in each of the scenarios and then draw or write about yourself doing just that.

SWEET DREAMS

Sometimes the issues bothering us in the day visit us at night.

Use this page to jot down any dreams where you think your subconscious might be telling you to be kinder or more generous.

HUG IT OUT

A hug is the embodiment of kindness and can be a great way to show someone you care.

Colour in a pair of bears every time you give a hug to someone who needs one.

THE BIT FOR GROWN UPS

This activity book is perfect for parents, teachers, learning mentors, caregivers and youth leaders who want to promote kindness and help children to develop a social conscience.

We all want the best for our children and one of the greatest gifts we can give them is that of a global conscience. Inspiring our children to be curious about the world and to become globally aware helps them to thrive and become responsible, caring individuals, ready to work with others to have a positive impact on the planet. To help our children to become global citizens, we must teach them from a young age to appreciate, communicate and interact with people across different cultures and in other countries. We must talk to them about the issues that affect humanity and our planet and encourage empathy.

It is possible to encourage your child to have a more global viewpoint merely by introducing them to different people and experiences. Even if extensive travel is not within reach, there is much you can do on your own doorstep to help your child to discover the world. Sit in front of a world atlas and pore over continents and countries. Introduce your child to food, literature, music, art and history. Meet people from different cultures and talk to your child about any differences and similarities they notice. You could advocate for foreign language learning in your child's school – and even model welcoming and inclusive behaviour by hosting a foreign student in your home.

The more you open your child's eyes, ears and mind to the fact that they exist as a part of a wider world, the more likely it is that they will grow to see themselves as connected with and integral to that world.

At the most basic level, promote kindness. Teach your child to be kind to themselves, to others who inhabit the world and to the planet itself.

These are just some of the amazing resources that will help you and your child to tap into the movement towards global citizenship...

WWW. GLOBALCITIZEN.ORG

This well-presented and accessible website features online petitions on the most pressing global issues, insightful articles on various campaigns, and ways to use your voice and online presence to raise awareness.

WWW.UNICEF.ORG

This is a great way to introduce children to the issues affecting children across the globe. It's a fantastic place to find out about children's rights, and to learn about protection, inclusion and equality initiatives.

WWW. THEWORLDKINDNESSMOVEMENT .ORG

This site contains all you need to know about The World Kindness Movement. It has information on World Kindness Day and how to list your city as a 'World Kindness City'. It's a great place to go to find some good, positive news and initiatives.